Human Rights

FOOD

Scarlett MccGwire

Wayland

Titles in the Human Rights series

Clean Environment

Food

Freedom of Expression

Homeland

Justice

Cover illustrations: *background* Healthy foodstuffs available to certain people in the world; *inset* Father and son, poor and hungry in California, USA.

© Copyright 1993 Wayland (Publishers) Ltd

Editor: Deborah Elliott
Designer: Joyce Chester

British Cataloguing in Publication Data
MccGwire, Scarlett
Food. – (Human rights)
I. Title II. Series
641.3
ISBN 0-7502-0643-8

Typeset by Dorchester Typesetting Group Ltd
Printed and bound by Rotolito Lombarda S.p.A., Milan

First published in 1993 by
Wayland (Publishers) Ltd
61 Western Road, Hove
East Sussex BN3 1JD
England

Picture acknowledgements

Format 10 (Jenny Matthews), 12 (Maggie Murray), 13 (Maggie Murray), 21 (Jenny Matthews), 22 (Maggie Murray), 26 (Maggie Murray), 32 (Ulrike Preuss), 33 (Stephanie Henry); Hutchison Library 5 (top), 9; Impact cover and title page (Stephen Shames/Visions), 5 (bottom, Michael George), 6 (Rune Eraker), 7 (Peter Menzel), 11 (Brian Harris), 14 (top, Piers Cavendish) (bottom, Sergio Dorantes), 15 (Ben Edwards), 16 (Peter Menzel), 18 (Mohamed Ansar), 19 (Mohamed Ansar), 20 `(Moradabadi), 23 (Caroline Penn), 24 (Ana C. Gonzales), 25 (Piers Cavendish), 27 (Rupert Conant), 29 (Christopher Cormack), 30 (Colin Jones), 31 (David Lurie), 34 (Jeremy Nicholl), 36 (Peter Arkell), 37 (Mohamed Ansar), 38 (Joe Fish/Reflex), 40 (Caroline Penn), 42 (Piers Cavendish); Photofusion 8 (Ingrid Garshon), 28 (J. Southworth), 35 (Gina Glover); Popperfoto 17 (top) (bottom, Reuter), 39, 43 (Reuter); Science Photo Library 41 (CNRI); Skjold 4; Tony Stone Worldwide cover background (Jim Cambon).

Contents

It should be emphasized that although the material in this book is derived from the experiences of real people in real situations, the characters themselves are fictitious and should not therefore be seen to be representing the experiences of particular persons.

1

The right to live

PAUL is thirteen years old. He lives with his mother in a one-room apartment in Toronto in Canada. Paul's father left when Paul was six. Since then, Paul and his mother have lived on the money she earns working as a waitress. They have enough money to pay the rent – just. There is very little left over to pay bills or to buy food and clothes.

Paul's mother brings home scraps of food from the restaurant she works in, when she can. However, if she is caught doing this, she will lose her job. Paul cannot remember the last time he ate a proper meal. He can only remember feeling hungry.

Theresa is also thirteen years old. She lives on the island of Negros, which is one of the 7,000 islands of the Philippines. Most people in Negros work on the many sugar plantations on the island.

In the 1980s, the world price of sugar fell. As a result, many of the sugar plantations on Negros were closed. Theresa's father was one of the unlucky people who lost their jobs. He has not been able to find work since.

Theresa's family has no money to buy food. Her family, like many families in Negros, is starving. Theresa's mother grows some vegetables in the family's garden, but these are not enough to feed everyone.

Paul is thirteen years old. He lives in Toronto, which is the second largest city in Canada. Paul does not have enough to eat.

Left Thirteen year-old Theresa tries to smile for the camera. Theresa lives in Negros, which is one of the 7,000 islands that make up the Philippines. Theresa does not have enough to eat.

Below Some people in the world have more food than they could possibly need. They can enjoy ice-cream and sweets, and other luxuries. Yet others have very little food, or even no food at all. Do you think this is fair?

Theresa is undernourished and, as a result, is becoming very ill. If her situation does not change soon, Theresa could become very ill indeed.

Paul and Theresa are from different families and were born in different countries. Both are hungry. Do you think they deserve to be hungry?

Hopefully your answer is no. If it is, then you have recognized Paul and Theresa's right to food.

We do not have a choice about the circumstances into which we are born. Whether our families are rich or poor, or whether we are born in Canada or the Philippines is a matter of chance. This means that inequalities and unfairnesses exist. While Paul is hungry and Theresa is starving, other people are throwing food away because they have too much.

Food is the most basic right any human on this planet can demand. It is the energy of life. Without food people would and, sadly, all too frequently do, die.

It seems obvious that the first requirement of any government should be to make sure that all its people are fed. However, not one country in the world has achieved this. Paul and Theresa are not alone – there have never been so many hungry people as now. Enough food is produced in the world to feed everyone, yet every night 700 million people – one-sixth of the world's population – go to bed hungry.

The United Nations (UN) is an organization with representatives from all the world's governments. In 1948, members of the UN drew up a set of rules on human rights by which all countries and peoples could live together peacefully and fairly without injustice and inequality. This set of rules is called the 'Universal Declaration of Human Rights'.

According to Article 25 of the Declaration, 'Everyone has the right to a standard of living adequate (good enough) for the health and well-being of himself and of his family, including food, clothing, housing and medical care. . .'

Although most countries have agreed to the list, almost all have failed to abide by any of the rules. If a country puts forward a policy that denies members of its population food, then that country is failing to uphold its people's human rights. The governments of Canada and the Philippines have denied Paul and Theresa's human rights, not by causing them to

Patients in a hospital in Kapoeta, in southern Sudan, suffering from malnutrition (lack of foods needed for health and growth).

be without food, but by failing to provide them with food, or the opportunity to have enough money to buy food which is 'adequate' for their 'health and well-being'.

In the following chapters, we shall look at some of the ways in which governments and charity organizations can help, and are helping to prevent hunger. We shall also see how hungry people are working to feed themselves.

We shall look at some of the causes of hunger and starvation. Most people who are denied the right to food live in developing countries. The rising population in places such as Brazil, Ethiopia and Thailand is often blamed for the hunger and malnutrition in those countries. People suffer from malnutrition when they do not get enough foods with vitamins and minerals, which are important for health and growth.

Rising populations are certainly part of the problem. Floods, drought, war and other natural disasters also contribute to hunger. However, the key is poverty. All over the world, millions of people go hungry because they do not have the money to buy food or the land on which to grow it. Millions more have a poor diet, normally because they cannot afford a better one. They are more likely to suffer heart disease, food-related cancers, teeth decay and bowel disorders.

In rich and poor countries all over the world, millions of people are hungry because they do not have the money to buy food.

More than 1 billion people in the world live in absolute poverty, surviving on £175 or less per person each year. That is what the average person in the USA, Australia and the UK spends on eating out in restaurants every year. For those 1 billion people, inequality exists.

In Bangladesh 10 per cent of people who own land control 50 per cent of the land and 50 per cent of cattle. Over half the number of people living in the countryside in Bangladesh have no land at all. In the UK, fewer people own most of the land. However, people in the UK are better fed because, generally, they have more money.

Developed countries acknowledge their people's right to food. They have welfare systems (see page 27) which were set up to make sure everyone had enough money to live and eat. However, there are still a lot of hungry people in these countries, particularly those living on benefits.

In developing countries, the right to food might seem to be the same as the right not to go hungry. Certainly that is the first and most obvious requirement. However, we should all have the right to eat decent, healthy food. In chapter 7 of this book, we see what is being done, and unfortunately more often not being done, to give us safe and healthy food.

Food affects our health and the quality of our lives. Nowhere can we see this more clearly than in developing countries when famine strikes. In ten developing countries, 230 out of every 1,000 children die before the age of five. This is almost one-quarter of the children. They often die from disease, rather than starvation. However, because they do not have enough to eat, the children are not strong enough to fight off disease.

Most people have enough to eat. This book tells the stories of different peoples who have been denied this basic right. Many of the stories are distressing, but they show people with dignity who, despite terrible problems,

are trying to help themselves and each other. Hunger and starvation are not just about starving children in refugee camps awaiting parcels of food. Neither are they just about people supposedly preferring to live on the streets rather than get jobs, because they are 'scroungers' or 'lazy'. If we believe that humans have any rights at all, then we must believe they have the right to food. It is the basis of life.

Ray lives in Durham, a middle-class town in the north-east of England. Ray has spent years living in institutions. Until recently, Ray was living in a hostel, but it was closed down. Now, Ray lives on the streets and hunts through litter bins in search of scraps of food.

2

Famine

MILLIONS of people in the world suffer from the effects of famine. Millions more do not receive enough food or have poor diets.

The media (television, newspapers and magazines) devote more coverage to famine than to lack of food or poor diets in developing countries. This is because the images connected with famines – people suffering from a severe lack of food – are much more shocking and appalling. Famines are often the result of a newsworthy disaster – war or drought, for example.

Most food comes from farming, which is dependent on the weather. When there is a drought, or too much rain, or a particularly bad winter in developing countries, there will usually be a shortage of food. There are lots of people competing for the food, so prices go up. This is bad news for people caught in the poverty trap, but most are able to find some food somewhere. If a food shortage occurs in developing countries there is a famine, and people starve.

Ahmed is fourteen years old. He lives in the North Dafur region of Sudan with his mother. His father works in Libya as an unskilled labourer.

Ahmed says, 'People began moving to our village in 1984 and 1985. Those were the years of the terrible drought.

Ahmed lives in the North Dafur region of Sudan. There is not enough food to feed everyone in Ahmed's village. Many people in Ahmed's village are starving to death.

Everyone's crops died and there was barely enough water to drink. People came here and to other villages and towns to be close to water supplies and other services. Now there are so many people in our village that soon there won't be enough food and water for everyone.'

Ahmed and his mother used to grow millet and many kinds of vegetable on their farm. After the harvest the crops were stored in a big cellar under the ground. The stored grain was not to be used except in emergencies. In 1990 there was an emergency – the crop failed. The cost of grain went up to twenty times the usual price.

Ahmed goes on, 'Our stocks are almost all used up. Even if we had enough money to buy grain, there is hardly any in the market.' Ahmed's basic diet is asida – a kind of porridge made of millet flour. Usually okra (a vegetable), or tomato and onion sauce is added to it, but Ahmed cannot get these. He and his mother have to use Mukhait berries instead, which are bitter and not very nice.

Many parts of the Sudan have been affected by drought – year after year of little or no rainfall. Farmers have been unable to grow their crops, so vast areas of land lie dry and barren.

'I had to leave school because mother could not afford to keep me there. I look after some goats. We had to sell one and will probably have to sell the other four too. My mother collects wood to sell in the market. The price is low, so she can only make about five Sudanese pounds (80 pence) a day. Soon there will be no money for food. I don't know what we will do.'

The terrible famine in Sudan in 1984/5 has its roots in history. In 1898 the British ruled Sudan and the country's farmers were taxed and made to grow cotton for sale to other countries. Workers were paid very little and were often given food instead of money.

This is the El Fasher refugee camp in Sudan. Hungry people from all over the country come here hoping to find food. There are many people in Sudan and only a limited supply of available food. This means that the people selling food can charge very high prices.

When Sudan became independent in 1956, the economy still depended on cotton. A small number of people in the north of the country continued the British policies. This led to an increase in the feelings of hostility between people in the north and the poorer south, already divided by culture and religion. A long-running civil war began.

When the world price of cotton fell, the Sudanese government turned to sorghum as a cash crop. Many cattle herders, nomads and farmers were put off their land by large farming companies, which borrowed money from developing countries to buy up land. Soon Sudan found itself with a huge debt. To raise money, the government put up the price of grain. When drought struck in the 1980s, people could not afford to buy food. The result was famine. The people of Sudan could grow enough food, but as war and a failing economy continue to take their toll, people like Ahmed and his mother are again gripped by a famine not of their own making.

As many as 27 million people face desperate food shortages in Africa, over half of them are children. The causes vary from country to country. But for many people, it is a lethal combination of factors – civil war, year after year of drought and economic collapse – that has fuelled the famines which bring ordinary families, like Ahmed's, to the brink of disaster.

Sula remembers the long and bitter civil war, when the people of Eritrea fought for independence (to be separate) from Ethiopia.

Buying weapons

The amount of money governments spend on the military is often said to be a major cause of famine in many countries. In fact, statistics prove that the least developed countries spend proportionally less on their armed forces than most developed countries. Nevertheless, in the last twenty-five years, the percentage of money spent on the military by governments of developing countries has doubled. More money has been spent on weapons and the army than on health and education.

Sula lives in a village in Eritrea, a province in northern Ethiopia. The people of Eritrea fought to make their country independent. There was a bitter civil war between the EPLF – a guerrilla army of Eritrean rebels – and the Ethiopian government.

Sula's father was a farmer. He also grew okra and cabbage on a plot of land next to the family farm. The civil war had a devastating effect on Sula and her family.

Sula explains, 'Soldiers came to our village looking for guerrillas (EPLF). They (the Ethiopian soldiers) trampled across the land and destroyed the crops. The soldiers took my dad away. They beat him very badly. They wanted dad to give information about the EPLF, but dad didn't know anything.

'There was a lot of fighting in the village. Dad was frightened that we might be killed, so we had to leave the farm and go to live with my aunt and uncle in another village. There was no work in their village. We had no food and no money to buy food. No one in the village had any food. I used to dream of having a full stomach, but it never happened.'

Why was Sula hungry? There was food in Ethiopia, yet millions of people were starving. The government sold food to other countries in order to raise money to buy weapons. These weapons were given to soldiers to be used against the EPLF. Many of the weapons were seized by members of the EPLF, who in turn used them against the Ethiopian soldiers. The war continued as a result, which meant the Ethiopian government needed more money to buy weapons.

This may sound confusing to you. It certainly does to Sula. She says, 'I feel so angry. I know people who died from lack of food. My father cannot walk properly. He got rickets because he didn't get enough vitamins. What good did the weapons do us?'

Refugees from the civil war in Ethiopia at the Wad Sherifee camp in Sudan. Sudan itself is plagued with problems of drought and civil war.

Overpopulation

Overpopulation occurs when too many people are living in a particular place, all using limited supplies of food and water.

Left A shanty town in Guatemala City, Guatemala. There are so many people living in the city that there is a problem with overcrowding. Many people have to live in makeshift shelters.

Below In places of extreme poverty, like Mexico City, it is not uncommon to find people picking through rubbish to find clothes, bits of furniture, or anything that could be put to some use.

Overpopulation is often given as a cause of famine in many of the countries in Africa, Asia, and Central and South America. Yet, there are many areas within Africa with very few people. Although almost 10 per cent of the world's population live in Africa, the continent has 20 per cent of the world's farmland.

There is little doubt that rising populations are a problem in some parts of the world. Brazil, in particular, has problems with overcrowding and also appalling poverty. However, the link between famine and overpopulation is slight. There are far more people per square metre in China and India than in Africa, yet, nowadays, famines are rare in both China and India.

A rapid rise in population in a country does not always mean there is less food for everyone. However, overpopulation creates problems when there is a huge difference between the rate the population is growing and the development of services such as water, transport and health. This huge difference occurs in some African countries.

This irrigation system in India was set up to carry water to places of low rainfall.

3

War

THERE are always a number of reasons why wars happen. There is always one result of which we can all be certain – innocent people suffer. War is one of the major causes of hunger in the world.

The civil war in Somalia has raged for the past ten years. This has meant that very little food is grown and crops are often burnt by one side or the other. People in Somalia are starving. Emergency food has been sent by other countries. Convoys of lorries carrying the food have difficulty reaching towns and villages because they are attacked. The USA has sent an army to Somalia to make sure the food convoys reach the hungry people. However, this hasn't stopped the civil war or the killings.

In 1991 war broke out in former Yugoslavia between the states which made up the country. After bitter fighting the country was split into small republics: Bosnia-Herzegovina, Croatia, Slovenia and Serbia. The fighting has made it difficult for food and medical supplies to reach some areas.

'Technicals' or 'Mad Maxes' are the names given to the Toyota jeeps with anti-aircraft guns, which are used in street warfare in Mogadishu in Somalia. While the fighting continues, the people of Somalia grow hungrier.

A young Somali boy runs towards a relief convoy bringing much-needed food to his village. In the background a French soldier stands poised, ready to defend the safe arrival of the food.

In fact, United Nations convoys carrying food supplies have been deliberately attacked. Lack of supplies has forced people to leave their homes in search of food. Many are starving.

In a war, many people suffer. This prisoner of war hands out soup to other Muslim and Croatian inmates. They are being held in a Serbian-controlled detention camp in Manjaca, Bosnia.

In 1990, Iraqi soldiers, led by Saddam Hussein, invaded Kuwait. The UN declared that sanctions should be imposed against Iraq to make them leave Kuwait. The sanctions meant that ships were prevented from entering Iraqi ports and all trade with Iraq was banned. The result was war between Iraq and the rest of the world. This war was known as the Gulf War.

The war ended in 1991. Although Iraq was defeated, Saddam refused to agree to the UN terms for peace, so, sanctions were not lifted. While world leaders threatened their country, the ordinary people of Iraq suffered because of a war which they had never wanted.

Um Hameth lives in Baghdad, the capital city of Iraq. Her husband died in 1988. Since then, Um has brought up her two children alone. She has struggled to make ends meet.

Um says, 'The government gave everyone ration cards. We can use the cards to buy food at a reasonable price for about twelve days in every month. When this food runs out, I have to buy more – but the price of everything is about twenty times more than I pay with the ration card.'

Um bakes her own bread, which she sells or gives to friends and neighbours. All of Um's money is spent on food. There is nothing left over to buy clothes or to pay the rent. Um goes on, 'I have had to borrow money from relatives.

The war has been over for a few years, but things are just getting worse. I don't even know what the war was really about. I feel very frightened for my children. I don't know for how much longer I can give them food.'

Eighteen million people live in towns and cities in Iraq. Many, like Um and her family, suffer food shortages.

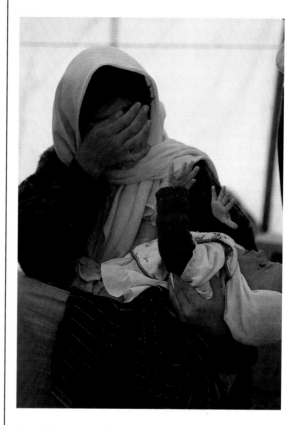

Um Hameth hides her face from the camera. She is weeping because her children are hungry and she cannot feed them. The Gulf War has left Iraq with a serious food shortage. Food that is available is very expensive. Um struggles to make ends meet. She does not know how much longer she can keep going.

The areas most affected are the Shia areas in the south of the country and the Kurdish regions of the north. The basic essentials of life (food and water) are a struggle.

Before the Gulf War, the people of Iraq had suffered nearly ten years of war with neighbouring Iran. About one million people were killed on both sides. Many Iraqis were killed during the Gulf War. There was also a great deal of damage to the country.

The UN has insisted that trade sanctions continue against Iraq. This has meant that towns and cities, destroyed during years of bombing, have not been rebuilt. However, the sanctions have affected the ordinary people most.

In the past, 70-80 per cent of the food in Iraq was bought from other countries. Since the Gulf War, the amount of food produced in Iraq has fallen by 80 per cent. This has led to huge food shortages. Unfortunately, because there is less food, which means there is a higher demand, prices are very high. In fact, food costs about fifty times more than before the Gulf War, yet wages have gone down.

Abu Zaynab is a cattle farmer who lives close to Al-Amarah in the south of Iraq. Abu used to support his family by rearing calves. In December 1991, he had to sell the herd. The price of the food he bought to feed the cattle

These are Abu Zaynab's children. They help their father to try to earn enough money to buy food. The sanctions against Iraq have not been lifted. Saddam Hussein and his government do not seem to be changing. The future looks very bleak for Abu and the children.

had risen by 400 per cent. Now, Abu and his children look after their neighbour's four cows. They also grow a small amount of wheat – not enough to live on. Abu has no money to buy food for his family. Abu speaks for many Iraqi people when he says, 'I do not know what the future will bring. If something does not happen, many, many people will die of hunger.'

Kurdish people in Iraq demonstrate about the harsh treatment they receive from the government of their own country.

Since 1979, the government of Iraq has spent most of its time at war or preparing for war. In 1991, the government spent almost one-third of all the money it earned (from taxes and so on) on the military. This is a greater proportion than any other country in the world. Meanwhile the people of Iraq grow hungrier.

The average diet for women has fallen from 2,500 calories before the war, to 1,000 calories. However, as always, children have been most affected. In 1990, 1 per cent of all Iraqi children did not have enough to eat. By 1992, the figure had risen to 25 per cent; 10,000 children had died of hunger. The numbers are still rising. A journalist who visited Iraq in 1992 summed up the link between war and hunger: 'The bombing has stopped but the killing goes on.'

4

Overcoming famine

A great deal is being done to deal with the root causes of famine – it just does not make television news.

The charities and other groups helping developing countries are known as Non-Governmental Organizations (NGOs) because they are independent of any government. NGOs do not just send aid, they look for long-term solutions to the problems of hunger and famine, such as helping farmers to become self-sufficient. This means farmers can grow their own food and not need help from anyone else.

Governments in African countries most affected by famine are also working to develop greater self-sufficiency, particularly in agriculture. For example, the production of sorghum and millet (cereals) in Sudan increased by 28 per cent over a five-year period in the 1980s. The production of cereal and pulses (beans, lentils and so on) increased by 31 per cent in Ethiopia over the same period of time.

In The Gambia, as in most of Africa, two-thirds of food production is the responsibility of women. Nakadeli is fourteen. Her mother, Soto, is president of the food production group in Dobbo.

Nakadeli says, 'The rains here are really unpredictable. But this year has been good. Because we planted our crops early, we made sure we did not waste a drop of rain. The horse and plough mean that we can do work in less than half the time it would normally take by hand.'

A joint Oxfam and Save the Children (NGOs) trucking operation, which delivered relief supplies of food and medicine to villages in Ethiopia.

Everyone in Nakadeli's village helps to clear the land of trees to make it suitable for ploughing.

'We do it by hand rather than burning the bush. That would destroy the trees which protect the soil and plants from bad weather.'

Lines of women cut and chop the thick grasses, bushes and smaller trees. These are collected by the younger children and then carefully burned to be ploughed back into the soil. The ashes contain important minerals which are good for the soil. After sowing, the women look after the crop, keeping it clear of weeds. At harvest time, the whole village works together to bring in the crops.

Nakadeli explains, 'We store the crops – corn and rice – on the roofs. I'm sure our roof will collapse, there's so much food up there. The groundnuts are stored in huge piles around the compound.'

The horse, plough and seeder were supplied on an interest-free loan by an NGO. The money will be repaid from the sale of part of the crop from the next few harvests.

Nakadeli and the other women in Dobbo have worked hard to make sure everyone in the village has food. They spend days clearing fields for planting. The women also look after the crops until harvest time. Then, everyone in the village helps to bring in the crops.

Regular nutrition classes are held at this hospital in Uganda. People can come along to ask questions and get important advice about which foods are important for health and growth.

'We want to pay the money back. It is very good of people to help us, but we want to help ourselves too.'

The major charities around the world are all involved in long-term development work. They are providing families in Mozambique with seeds and tools to plant and grow food. They have helped farmers in Ethiopia to build mountain terraces to prevent soil erosion.

Not all aid projects are as successful as Nakadeli's. In a crisis, when war, flooding or drought cause serious food shortages by disrupting production, emergency aid in the form of food is desperately needed to help tide people over until the next harvest.

For many governments of rich countries, food aid is convenient: it is unwanted food. Many of these countries have stockpiles of certain foods, called 'mountains'. The 'mountains' are often destroyed to keep the price of that food high. Almost half the food contribution to developing countries from Europe is milk powder and butter oil. Both these are 'mountains'.

Foodstuffs such as milk powder and butter oil can cause problems. Diets of local people can change overnight and donated food can flood the market, lowering the price of grain and forcing local farmers out of business. Less food is grown so more aid is needed. Communities – even countries – can become dependent on food aid.

The 'baby milk scandal'

Perhaps the most obvious example of how developing countries can be exploited is the 'baby milk scandal'.

Nestlé is a large company. One of its products is powdered milk for babies. Nestlé has been trying to sell this milk in developing countries for many years. Its attempts have been very successful – for company profits, not for the babies.

For a lot of mothers in developing countries, the Nestlé baby milk was a disaster. Many hospitals did not have facilities to clean the bottles; often there was no hot water. Some babies became ill. The milk was very expensive. This meant that mothers were tempted to add more water to it, to make the milk go further. Some babies were undernourished, as a result.

In 1988, £10 million of baby milk was sent to Pakistan. About 4.5 million baby bottles are sold in Pakistan each year. Yet, bottle feeding is the major cause of diarrhoea in babies.

Around 20,000 babies in Pakistan die from diarrhoea every year. Between 1981 and 1991, 9 million babies in developing countries died as a result of bottle feeding.

People in developing countries should not have to rely on food from overseas organizations. The problem is, how do they achieve their right to food, themselves?

These women belong to the San Lorenzo community in Lempira, Honduras. Members grow enough maize, beans and vegetables to feed all 500 people in the community. They are working together to help themselves.

Many countries affected by drought have managed to develop their economic resources to help them through difficult periods. India, for example, has a national food security system, whereby food and money are set aside for use in an emergency. This means that major droughts, such as the drought that affected India between 1987 and 1989, do not now lead to famine. The Indian government can tackle the drought without help from abroad. Indeed, India is now in a position to provide aid to African countries.

Botswana and a number of other drought-prone countries in Africa have managed to avoid famine. The governments have managed to build up economic resources to help people during difficult periods. They have schemes such as free food distribution, extra food for school children and cash for work projects.

Food security is the key to overcoming famine. It means that people should have enough food to lead active and healthy lives. Food security can be provided in two ways: making sure there is always an adequate supply of available food, by producing it locally or importing (buying) it from other countries; and enabling people to produce food themselves and to buy it. In much of Africa, people have no food security whatsoever.

Women and children from the San Lorenzo community work hard to prepare the land for planting.

Food insecurity does not necessarily lead to famine. Famines are actually rare, though much of the area of Africa around the Sahara Desert is affected by drought. People get by, adapting their farming to low rainfall, making use of local foods, such as wild fruits and vegetables, and helping each other in times of need.

The real problem is a 'food crisis'. This is when there is no food available, and people are no longer able to cope. This is what we see on television screens and read about in newspapers concerning famine in Africa.

The strongest message about the current food crisis in Somalia in Africa, is that assistance from other countries was too little and came too late. Despite repeated warnings from many NGOs in late 1990 that a crisis was looming, only a tiny amount of the food needed was sent. Few countries responded immediately to the early warning signals.

It is just as important to build up the long-term food security of those countries prone to famine. This can be achieved by putting money into developing new farming methods and by developing stable economies and reliable public services.

There are enough resources in the world to make sure that every single child has food security. The governments of all countries must make sure that food security, rather than food crisis, is a reality.

In order to achieve food security, millions of pounds would have to be spent on developing farming and agricultural equipment, and developing the economies of particular countries. The role of the international community is vital. It has to help provide the right conditions for food security: peace, stability, economic growth and a reduction in the huge debts facing many developing countries.

However, although the countries in the international community seem to

This village blacksmith in Burkina Faso was trained as part of a rural development scheme. Money for the scheme was supplied by an international NGO.

agree with the 'Universal Declaration of Human Rights', once again the idea seems more acceptable than the reality. The food policies of the UK and the USA, for example, are to do with trade and making money. They are not about providing food for the world or even food for their own people. Their policies add to the problem of hunger.

5

Poverty

IT is not just developing countries where people go hungry. In Europe, Canada, USA and Australia, many people simply do not have enough money to buy food.

Many developed countries have some sort of welfare system. This is a scheme organized by governments in particular countries. Welfare systems were set up to make sure that people had enough to eat, a roof over their heads and enough money to live on. They apply to all the people in a country, no matter who they are, where they live or if they have jobs.

The welfare system in the UK was set up in 1948. Surveys have shown that between 1982 and 1992, the welfare system failed. The gap between rich and poor people in the UK has widened. In 1988, the British government passed the 'Social Security Act'. The Act means that sixteen and seventeen year olds cannot claim any income support. The government made it clear that people of this age should be living at home, or earning some kind of living through a Youth Training Scheme (YTS) or a job. However, young people are often forced to leave home. They need help and understanding not punishment.

In the USA, poor people are getting poorer. One out of every ten people in the USA depends on free food stamps just to get enough to eat.

France is one of the wealthiest countries in Europe. Yet not everyone in the country enjoys the benefits of the wealth. This woman in Nice is begging for money to buy some food.

Rob is seventeen years old. He lives on the streets of San Diego in southern California. Rob says, 'I was never very good at school. When I left, I had no qualifications and I couldn't get a job. My dad threw me out of the house. He said if I couldn't get a job then he wasn't going to support me.

'I moved here to San Diego because it's a big city and I thought it would be easy to find work. But no one will employ me because I haven't got a permanent address. I can't afford to rent an apartment because I haven't got a job. I can't get any benefits (welfare payments from the government) because they (social service officials) say I should go back home to live.'

Living on the streets and begging for food in London, England.

Rob hasn't got any money. During the day he sits outside banks in the city and begs for money. The police and bank officials keep moving him on.

Rob is speaking for many people living on the streets all over the world when he says, 'I can't remember the last time I had a proper meal. Sometimes people are really nice and buy me a burger or a sandwich. They don't see me as a drunk or a layabout. They see that I've just been unlucky, and that it could happen to them. They can tell that I need food.

'I see pictures on billboards of people starving to death in Africa, but I'm starving here in the USA. Yet, it is the richest country in the world.'

During the 1980s, the government of the USA cut down the amount of money it spent on welfare. In the UK, the number of unemployed people (without jobs) went up dramatically in the early 1980s and again in the early 1990s. Although unemployed people receive benefits, living for a long period of time on a low income doesn't do anyone any good. The result was that many people suffered and the number of hungry people grew, in both the UK and the USA.

Welfare payments were cut in the USA because many politicians argued that some people simply saw the money as a way of not having to work. In Ohio, in the USA, welfare payments

Unemployed people can come along to this centre in Birmingham to meet other people in similar situations and to enjoy a hot meal. Many of these people do not have enough money to live on. The centre provides them with at least one good meal a day.

were cut to $100 (about £60) a month. People were only allowed to claim the money for six months of the year. This meant that 90,000 people had absolutely no money to live on for six months every year.

The state of Wisconsin showed its worries about people 'taking advantage' of welfare. It changed the rules so that a woman could only claim benefits for those children born after she started receiving the benefits. The new rules encouraged women receiving welfare to have more children. If they had more children, they would get more money. The state of Wisconsin was encouraging people to 'take advantage'.

In Rob's case, he could not get welfare money because he did not have anywhere to live. This situation is also true in the UK. Landlords prefer to rent rooms to people with jobs. This means that people without jobs cannot find homes. People without homes cannot find jobs and cannot claim money to buy food. What has happened to their human rights?

The link between poverty, hunger, disease, famine and death in developing countries is all too clear. The link also exists in rich, developed countries, and this is becoming increasingly clear.

There are terrible examples of poverty in almost every country in the world. Brazil sells an enormous amount of food to other countries. Yet, seven out of ten children under five years of age in Brazil die of malnutrition. Over one-third of Brazilian people do not have enough to eat. Children in many parts of South and Central America do not get enough to eat.

Brazil is a huge country covering 8,511,965 sq km of land – almost half of the total land area in South America. There are many hungry mouths to feed, especially among young people. Almost half the population in Brazil is under the age of twenty. Most of the farmland in Brazil is owned by rich landowners. They grow single crops – coffee, sugar and soya – for sale to other countries. Large areas of land are left idle, out of the reach of landless people.

This photograph was taken in Manaus, a town in Brazil. The area is home to many families. The people are desperately poor – they simply do not have enough food to eat. They get by searching for scraps of food or by begging. Sometimes children are fed 'cakes' of wet newspaper.

The Landless Rural Workers Movement (MST) is an organization in Brazil. It was set up to give help and advice to people with small farms. If people live and grow food on unused land owned by rich landowners for one year and one day, by law they can stay on the land. After five years, the land belongs to the farmers. However, this hardly ever happens. The people are forced to leave the land and go back to being hungry and living in poverty.

Examples like these are often used by governments of developed countries when talking about 'problems' in developing countries. Many governments use these examples to hide the problems on their own doorsteps.

However, the number of people in the poverty trap in the USA, Australia, Canada and countries in Europe is growing all the time.

Annie is seventeen. She and her fourteen-month-old daughter, Vicky, live in one room in a hotel in Leeds, in the north of England. She has been placed in the hotel by the DSS, which pays the rent. Annie's room is very small. Annie cannot get a job because she is looking after Vicky.

Annie and her daughter live in a room in a hotel. Annie does not have a cooker or a fridge. She buys ready-cooked food, which is expensive and not very healthy.

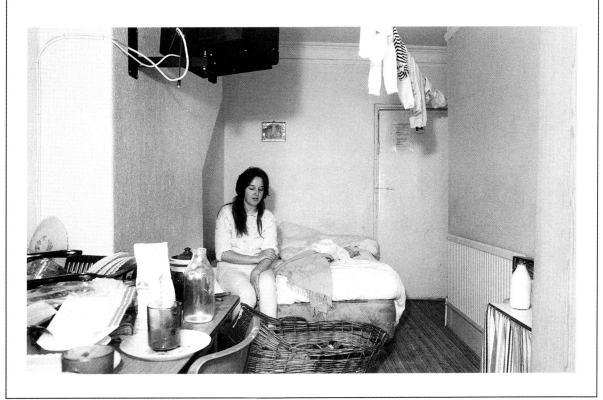

Annie says, 'I get £54.15 a week from the DSS (Department of Social Services). It's not really enough to live on, but we get by. That makes us luckier than a lot of people. Sometimes, though, there's only enough money to buy food for Vicky.

'I can remember quite a few times when I had nothing at all to eat for about two or three days at a time.'

The hotel rules mean that Annie cannot have a fridge in her room. This means she has nowhere to store food. Annie still feels lucky. 'I know lots of people who have to live like me. Some people aren't even allowed kettles in their rooms. They can't make a cup of tea. Those hotel owners are really mean. They don't want anyone to use electricity because it is included in the rent. The DSS pay the rent.'

Annie is worried about Vicky. Vicky always seems to be ill and isn't growing. Annie explains, 'She just isn't getting the proper food. Because I haven't got a fridge, I have to buy food in take-aways and cafes. I have tried to keep food cool on the window ledge, but this doesn't work very well, and it's useless in the summer.

'I hate complaining, though, because I know there are people a lot worse off than me. At least Vicky and I have a roof over our heads, and we do have money to buy some food. There are people living on the streets who have no food at all.'

Do you think Annie should feel lucky? She is hungry. Vicky is not getting proper food. Even though they are not starving to death, are their human rights being upheld?

All over the world, people are forced to look for ways to find food. Why should any one of us be hungry? Does anyone deserve to be hungry?

6

Diet

IN chapter 1, we looked at Article 25 of the 'Universal Declaration of Human Rights'. It said that everyone had the right to 'a standard of living' which looked after 'health and well-being'.

People who are starving or who do not have enough to eat have the right to food. We all have the right. We all have the right to eat reasonably healthy food too.

In the story about Annie and Vicky in the last chapter, we read how they did have food. However, it was not healthy food. Annie did not have much money – healthy food is usually expensive, especially in cities. Annie did not have anywhere to cook food. She and

Showing concern for someone in need. This woman is giving food and drink to homeless people in London on a bitterly cold evening.

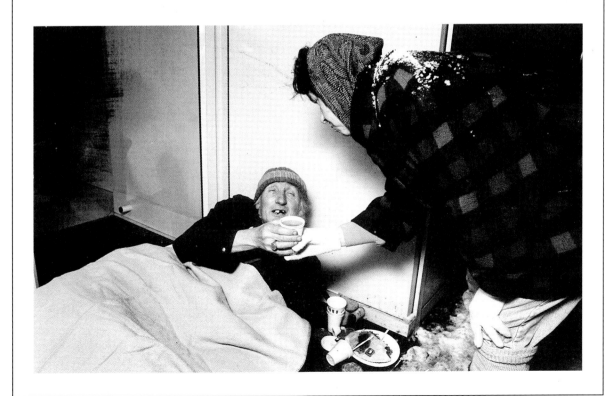

Vicky got food from takeaways and cafes – burgers, chips and processed food. Some processed food has lots of additives which are unhealthy.

Doctors in countries all over the world have prepared studies on junk foods. These are foods which have been pre-cooked – TV dinners, pot noodles, boil-in-a-bag meals, burgers, fried chicken, chocolate bars, crisps etc. The studies have shown that people who eat lots of junk food have low levels of nutrients, which are important for good health. Pregnant women who eat too much junk food have been proved to have babies who weigh less than the babies of women who eat fresh food.

Most of the studies in developed countries show that people who do not have much money tend to eat more junk food than wealthier people. This may seem strange to some of you. Why spend money on sweets and snacks instead of fruit and vegetables? A bag of sweets or a packet of crisps costs more than an apple or an orange.

Junk food is often very tasty, but is not necessarily healthy.

The reason is that it would cost much more to get the same amount of energy from fruit than from sweets. Sweets are full of carbohydrates, which give us energy. It is not healthy energy, especially for children. The energy only lasts for a short time and then children feel tired and bad-tempered.

Children need lots of energy. If they do not get enough, they become hungry and demand food. Sweets are very cheap ways of getting energy quickly.

The 1944 Education Act in the UK ruled that all school children should have a meal every day at school. This was to make sure that all children, no matter where they came from or how much money they had, would have at least one good meal a day. There were similar acts in other countries.

In 1988, the government in the UK changed the Act. Now, it is against the law for a child to have a free meal at school, unless the child's parent/s get income support (welfare payment).

When the Act was changed in 1988, 250,000 children in the UK could no longer have free meals. Jenny was one of those children.

Jenny is fourteen. She lives with her father, who works in a local factory. Jenny says, 'Dad doesn't earn very much. In fact, he would be better off on income support. He won't do that though. Dad likes having a job to go to – it makes him feel needed.'

Many children, like Peter and William, have burgers and chips almost every day. They should eat more vegetables and fresh food.

'We don't eat very healthily. Dad buys vegetables and fruit, but we eat a lot of fatty minced meat, because it's cheap. I used to really look forward to my school dinner. Even though it wasn't very nice sometimes, like when we got rice pudding, I knew it was good for me.

'When they changed the law, I had to ask dad for money to buy lunch. I feel awful, because I know that he doesn't have any money. Often he doesn't have any lunch himself. Sometimes I don't bother to ask him at all.

Sometimes Jenny does not get enough to eat.

I pretend I've got something. On those days I feel really hungry. I keep getting colds and the flu now. I know it's because I'm not getting the right food. Other kids at school go to the canteen and buy lots of different things. Their mums and dads must earn a lot of money. It's not fair.'

For many children, like Jenny, school meals used to provide the main meal of the day. In some schools, the price of the meals has gone up a lot. Many parents prefer to give their children packed lunches. This might not matter in a lot of schools where all the meals have chips with everything.

Young people living on poor diets are more likely to get illnesses like anaemia (lack of red blood cells), and chest infections. They are also more likely to fracture their bones because their bones do not develop properly.

A British survey, carried out during the 1980s, examined school children's diets. The results were so shocking, they took six years to be published. They showed that most school children in the UK did not get enough nutrients, like calcium or vitamins. Over 25 per cent of school children are too fat.

Although Jenny misses her free school meals, she is glad in some ways that she is no longer one of the children who get them. She explains, 'Lots of people tease the kids getting free meals. They call the kids scroungers.'

As we read in chapter 1, we cannot choose who we are, where we are born or who are our families. Some people have blue eyes, some have red hair, some have families who earn a lot of money. Do you think any of these make anyone better than anyone else? Sadly some people do.

Changes in eating habits

It has been proved that diet affects health. Television programmes, books and radio broadcasts have all looked at foods that make us ill, foods that cause allergies etc.

Many people have changed their diets to become more healthy. A survey carried out in the UK in 1986 showed that 86 per cent of adults had made some changes to their diets.

The results of the survey were as follows:

- 37 per cent of adults eat less processed meat;
- 57 per cent of adults eat less sugar;
- 27 per cent of adults eat more fruit and vegetables;
- 56 per cent of adults eat more wholemeal bread;
- 33 per cent of adults drink more low-fat milk;
- 56 per cent of adults grill rather than fry food.

The survey also showed that the people who eat most healthily are 'professional' (such as lawyers, doctors, writers, teachers, bank officials etc). Over twice as many people with manual jobs (plumbers, car mechanics, factory workers and building workers) eat unhealthily.

The main reason given for eating unhealthily was that healthy food is expensive. The second most important reason was pressure from other members of the family. Men are less likely than women to change to a healthy diet. Yet men often have the greatest say about what foods are served in families.

Statistics show that men are less likely than women to change to a healthy diet. Can you think of any reasons why this is so?

Many well-off people claim that poor people waste money on unhealthy food. They say that it is actually cheaper to eat healthy food.

In 1988 a test was carried out to see whether or not these claims were true. The test involved two shopping baskets, A and B. Basket A contained healthy food and B contained unhealthy food. Wherever people lived, it cost more to choose basket A, the healthy food. In poor areas, the healthy basket of food cost 20 per cent more than basket B, with the unhealthy food. What was even more alarming was that in very poor areas, it was impossible to buy some of the healthy food in basket A. The cost of an average 'healthy' basket of food was £33.49. The cost of an average 'unhealthy' basket of food was £28.57. Many young people on YTS schemes or income support have to buy food, clothes and toiletries (soap, toothpaste and so on), and pay bills out of £28 a week.

The 1988 test looked at two typical families – the Baxters and the Masons. Each family have four members. The Baxter family earned £230 a week, while the Mason family get £60.84 a week from income support. The Baxter family spend £33.72 a week on food, which is 14.7 per cent of their weekly budget. The Mason family spend £26.16 a week on food. This is 34 per cent of their weekly budget. Poor people know about the types of food to eat to have a healthy diet – many just cannot afford to buy these foods.

Selling unhealthy food to children

Selling food to children is big business. However, television advertising does not encourage children to eat heathily. In fact, television advertising has the opposite effect.

Most advertisements for food on children's television are for processed food, soft drinks, burgers and sweets. Although these foods are fairly unhealthy, the advertisements claim they are 'full of goodness', 'wholesome' or 'bursting with goodness'.

For people caught in the poverty trap, life can be very miserable.

7

Safe food

THE right to food includes the right to eat food that is safe. Safe food does not cause harm to the person who eats it. The desire to make money in today's society has meant that there are a number of different ways in which food can be made harmful for people to eat.

Most countries are affected by pollution. Factories dump waste into rivers and seas, damaging fish and plants.

The North Sea is one of the worst examples of polluted water in the world. Most of the waste is dumped at the mouth of the River Rhine and off the north coast of Brittany, in France.

Safe to eat? About 40,000 kg of fish died from water pollution in this river in Tainan, Taiwan. The river was polluted by rubbish from a local brewery, which is owned by the government.

Spraying crops with pesticides to kill any insects living on them. However, pesticides contain chemicals which can be harmful if they get into the food chain.

In 1986, a study was carried out by the Netherlands Institute for Fishery Investigations. Samples of flounder, dab and plaice (types of fish) were checked for levels of pollution. The study showed that 40 per cent of the fish had cancerous tumours or skin diseases and were not fit for people to eat. A similar study carried out in Germany showed that 42 per cent of fish were diseased.

In 1989, another study in the Netherlands discovered that fish contained traces of metals, such as mercury and cadmium, as well as pesticides. People in the Netherlands were advised to eat fish only once a week. Eels and fatty freshwater fish were to be avoided altogether.

In the USA, people were advised not to eat fish caught in polluted waters, or fish that feed from the sea or river beds in those areas.

Additives, flavourings and colourings are added to most processed foods. These make foods look and taste better, but are bad for our health.

Many farmers spray their crops with fertilizers, pesticides and insecticides. Fertilizers are used to make crops grow more quickly. Insecticides and pesticides are used to kill any insects that live on the crops. They all contain chemicals which can be harmful.

The most alarming examples of unsafe food are found in developing countries. In chapter 4, we read about the 'baby milk scandal' in Pakistan.

The company in question, Nestlé, was not aware that the baby milk would cause diarrhoea among babies. However, it was a case of a 'different' food type being introduced to a group of people without sufficient tests having been carried out to make sure it was safe.

DDT

DDT is an insecticide which was sprayed on crops in developed countries until tests showed it could harm humans if it entered the food chain. DDT got into the food chain in a number of ways. Crops sprayed with the insecticide were eaten by animals, which were then eaten by humans. Fruit and vegetables sprayed with DDT were eaten by humans, who perhaps did not wash them properly, or did not wash them at all.

DDT made people very ill, so it was banned. This left the companies which produced it with huge quantities of DDT. Many sold the insecticide to developing countries at cheap prices, with some catastrophic results. DDT caused deformity in new-born babies.

Water

The biggest threat to food safety in developing countries comes from water. We need water to live. However, water can carry horrific diseases and cause many deaths. World Health Organization (WHO) studies have shown that 80 per cent of diseases in the world today are caused by dirty water. These diseases claim the lives of over 30,000 children every day.

The diseases come from insects that breed in dirty water. In some places, this same water is used for drinking and cooking. The worst diseases are diarrhoea, malaria and bilharzia.

Bilharzia is caused by infected snails, which live in rivers, streams and lakes. The snails lay eggs which hatch into worms. The worms bore deep into the skin of humans and other mammals (elephants, dogs, cats, horses for example). The worms live in blood vessels, causing great misery, pain and weakness.

A bilharzia-carrying worm. The worm bores deep into the skin of mammals.

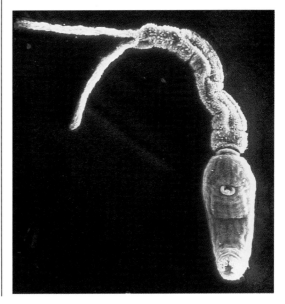

Bilharzia occurs mainly in rural areas in developing countries with very poor levels of hygiene. It can be introduced through irrigation schemes. These schemes are set up to help people by providing water in areas of low rainfall. However, if water containing infected snails is carried to a new area, then bilharzia is introduced to that area. WHO estimates that between 180,000,000 and 200,000,000 people in the world are infected by bilharzia.

Malaria is a disease carried by mosquitoes, which breed in stagnant ponds. It is common in hot, tropical countries.

Polio, cholera and dysentery (extreme case of diarrhoea) are all appalling diseases which cause suffering and death among huge numbers of people. In countries where water is scarce, the same water may be used for washing and watering animals and humans, for swimming, cooking and cleaning dishes and clothes. What else can people in these places do? If the only water they have is in a river or lake, what can they do? One solution is to boil water before drinking or cooking. However, the wider problems of sanitation (keeping things clean) and public health must be considered.

These women in El Salvador are collecting water from a burst water pipe. The water will be used for drinking and cooking.

This boy and his family are homeless: they live in a tent in California, USA. Their living conditions are poor and unhygienic. They have no running water and no toilet facilities.

Bawku is a district in northern Ghana. The period between May and June each year is known by local people as the 'hungry season'. In a year of poor rainfall or a bad harvest, the 'hungry season' is a time when people particularly suffer.

The 1991 'hungry season' was a time of particular suffering in Bawku. An outbreak of cholera swept through the area. Cholera is caused by bacteria in food or water. Sufferers develop extreme diarrhoea and vomiting.

The hospital in Bawku was filled with cholera patients. The local school building had to be turned into a temporary hospital. The disease claimed many lives in Bawku.

When the cholera outbreak was over, the people of Bawku tried to uncover the reasons why the disease had struck. It became clear that much of the food and water in the district were left uncovered. Flies, which carry the disease, could get to the food and water. Also, rubbish was often dumped close to food supplies, or in water used for drinking or cooking food. The people of Bawku undertook public health and environment safety schemes.

Public health and sanitation schemes are being introduced in many developing countries. This will mean that people have clean and safe water supplies.

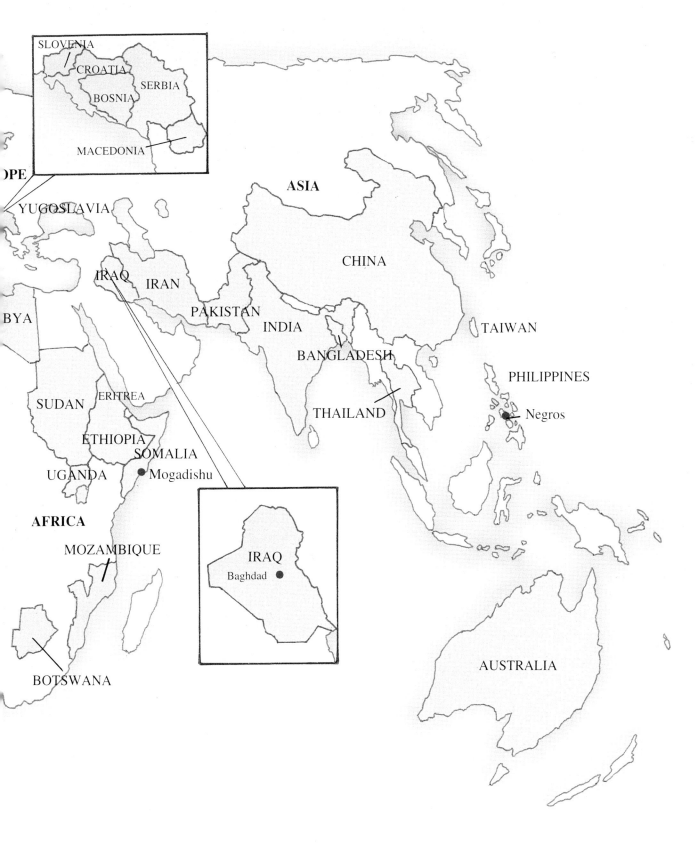

Glossary

Agriculture Farming the land.

Aid Help or assistance given to countries in times of crisis. The aid can be in the form of money, food, machinery, seeds etc.

Allergies Reactions to certain foods; some people come out in a rash when they eat shellfish or strawberries, for example.

Carbohydrates The sugars and starches found in foods.

Civil war A war between people who live in the same country.

Debt A sum of money owed by a person or country.

Drought A long period with a low rainfall.

Facilities Things that make actions possible or easier. For example, cooking facilities – kitchen, oven, power; cleaning facilities – bath, hot water, soap.

Famine A severe lack of food in an area or country.

Human rights If you have a 'right' to something, you can claim it as your own. We can all claim human rights – the rights we have from birth to adequate shelter, food, education, justice, freedom of expression, clean environment, and so on.

Independent When a state or country is independent, it is ruled by its own government and leaders and not by another country.

Interest-free loan Money which is loaned to a person or organization. The money is loaned on the understanding that only the same amount will be repaid.

Nutrients Substances found in certain foods which are good for our health.

Refugee Someone who has fled from his or her country and been accepted by the government of a new country.

Rickets A disease which softens and bends the bones. It is caused by a lack of vitamin D, which is found in certain foods.

Starvation Dying of hunger.

United Nations (UN) An organization, formed in 1945, which has almost all the states of the world as members. It acts to try to keep world peace, promote human rights and support development. The UN headquarters are in New York, USA.

Vitamins and minerals Substances found in foods such as milk, fruit, vegetables and fish. Vitamins and minerals are important for health and growth.

Further reading

Balances: a learning resource for food and nutrition courses at GCSE level (available from the Education Unit, Save The Children, Mary Datchelor House, 17 Grove Lane, London SE5 8RD)

Food or Famine? by Christopher Gibb (Wayland, 1987)

Human Rights by John Bradley (Franklin Watts, 1987)

Human Rights by David Selby (Cambridge University Press, 1989)

Human Rights by Jane Sherwin (Wayland, 1989)

Human Rights: Shelter by Kate Haycock (Wayland, 1993)

The Food Magazine (available from The Food Commission, 102 Gloucester Place, London W1)

Voices From Kurdistan ed. Rachel Warner (Minority Rights Group, 1991)

Voices From Eritrea ed. Rachel Warner (Minority Rights Group, 1991)

We Are What We Eat! by Heather Jarvis (UNICEF – UK, 1992)

Useful addresses

Australia
Australian Council for
Overseas Aid
PO Box 1562
Canberra, ACT, 2601

Human Rights Council of
Australia
PO Box 182
Glebe, NSW, 2037

Britain
Africa Watch
90 Borough High Street
London SE1 1LL

British Institute of Human Rights
Kings College, London
Faculty of Law
The Strand
London WC2R 2LS

Council for Education in
World Citizenship
Seymour Mews House
Seymour Mews
London W1H 9PE

The Minority Rights Group
379 Brixton Road
London SE11 4AA

The Refugee Council
3 Bondway
London SW8 1SF

Save The Children
Mary Datchelor House
17 Grove Lane
Camberwell
London SE5 8RD

UNICEF – UK
55 Lincoln's Inn Fields
London WC2A 3NB

Canada
Canada-Asia Working Group
11 Madison Avenue
Toronto
Ontario M5R 2S2

USA
International League for
Human Rights
432 Park Avenue.,S.,
Rm.1103
New York
NY 10016

Index